AF599197

# THE WASHINGTON COMMANDERS

BY ALICIA Z. KLEPEIS

EPIC

BELLWETHER MEDIA ★ MINNEAPOLIS, MN

**EPIC BOOKS** are no ordinary books. They burst with intense action, high-speed heroics, and shadows of the unknown. Are you ready for an Epic adventure?

This book is intended for educational use. Organization and franchise logos are trademarks of the National Football League (NFL). This is not an official book of the NFL. It is not approved by or connected with the NFL.

This edition first published in 2024 by Bellwether Media, Inc.

No part of this publication may be reproduced in whole or in part without written permission of the publisher. For information regarding permission, write to Bellwether Media, Inc., Attention: Permissions Department, 6012 Blue Circle Drive, Minnetonka, MN 55343.

Library of Congress Cataloging-in-Publication Data

Names: Klepeis, Alicia 1971- author.
Title: The Washington Commanders / by Alicia Z. Klepeis.
Description: Minneapolis, MN : Bellwether Media, 2024. | Series: Epic. NFL team profiles | Includes bibliographical references and index. | Audience: Ages 7-12 | Audience: Grades 2-3 | Summary: "Engaging images accompany information about the Washington Commanders. The combination of high-interest subject matter and light text is intended for students in grades 2 through 7"-- Provided by publisher.
Identifiers: LCCN 2023021978 (print) | LCCN 2023021979 (ebook) | ISBN 9798886874976 (library binding) | ISBN 9798886876857 (ebook)
Subjects: LCSH: Washington Commanders (Football team)--History--Juvenile literature. | Washington Football Team--History--Juvenile literature. | Washington Redskins (Football team)--History--Juvenile literature.
Classification: LCC GV956.W3 K54 2024 (print) | LCC GV956.W3 (ebook) | DDC 796.332/6409753--dc23/eng/20230522
LC record available at https://lccn.loc.gov/2023021978
LC ebook record available at https://lccn.loc.gov/2023021979

Text copyright © 2024 by Bellwether Media, Inc. EPIC and associated logos are trademarks and/or registered trademarks of Bellwether Media, Inc.

Editor: Kieran Downs Designer: Josh Brink

Printed in the United States of America, North Mankato, MN.

# TABLE OF CONTENTS

AN EXCITING ENDING ........ 4
THE HISTORY OF THE COMMANDERS ........ 6
THE COMMANDERS TODAY ........ 14
GAME DAY! ........ 16
WASHINGTON COMMANDERS FACTS ........ 20
GLOSSARY ........ 22
TO LEARN MORE ........ 23
INDEX ........ 24

# AN EXCITING ENDING

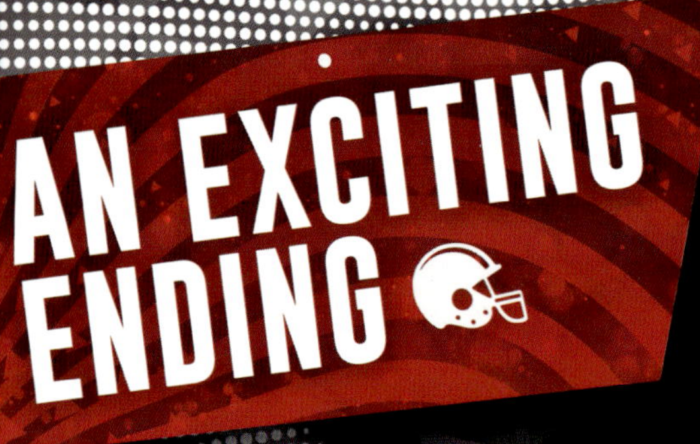

TAYLOR HEINICKE

In 2022, the Commanders face the Colts. The Colts are up 16–10 with less than one minute to go.

Commanders **quarterback** Taylor Heinicke throws a deep pass. It gets the Commanders to the 1-yard line. The next play, Heinicke runs for a **touchdown**! The Commanders go on to win!

# THE HISTORY OF THE COMMANDERS

The Washington Commanders first played in Boston, Massachusetts, in 1932. They were known as the Boston Braves.

In 1937, the team moved to Washington, D.C. They won the National Football League (NFL) **championship** that year. They won again in 1942.

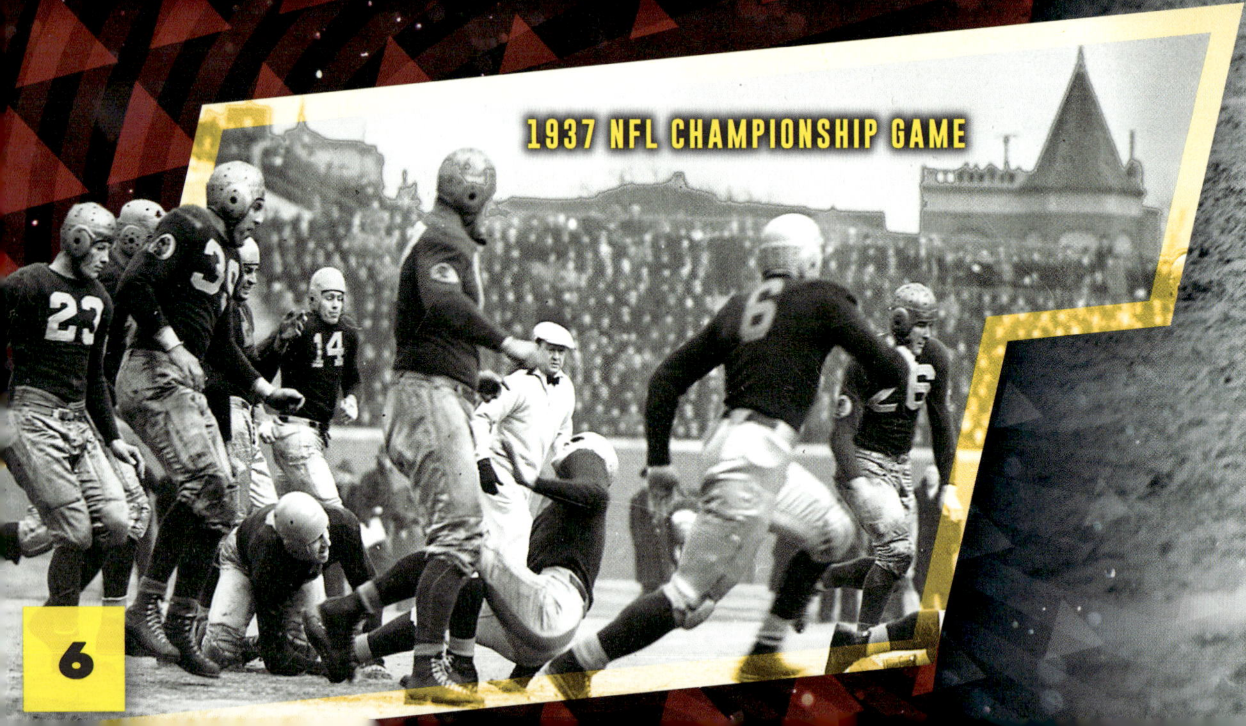

1937 NFL CHAMPIONSHIP GAME

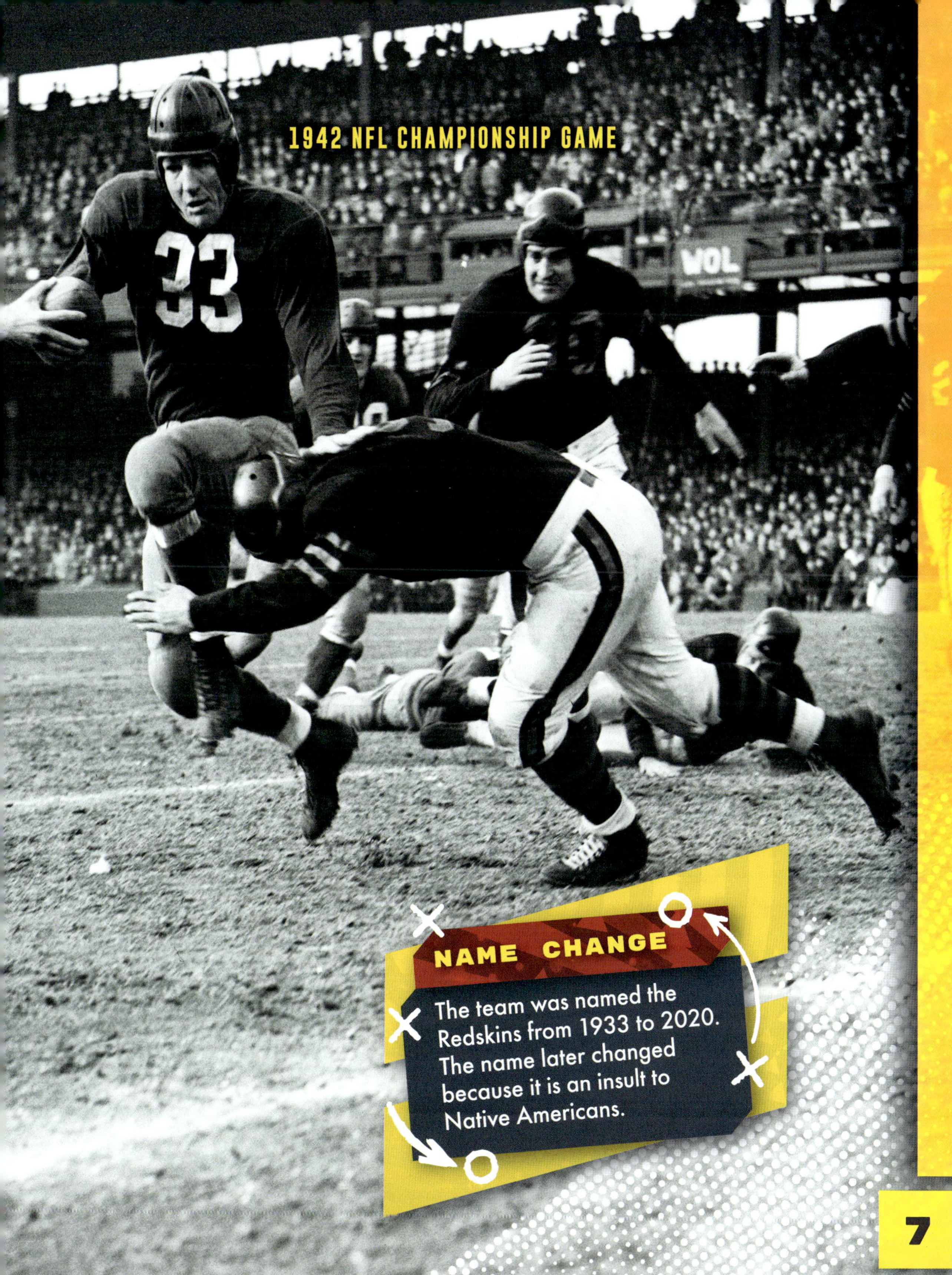


1942 NFL CHAMPIONSHIP GAME

## NAME CHANGE

The team was named the Redskins from 1933 to 2020. The name later changed because it is an insult to Native Americans.

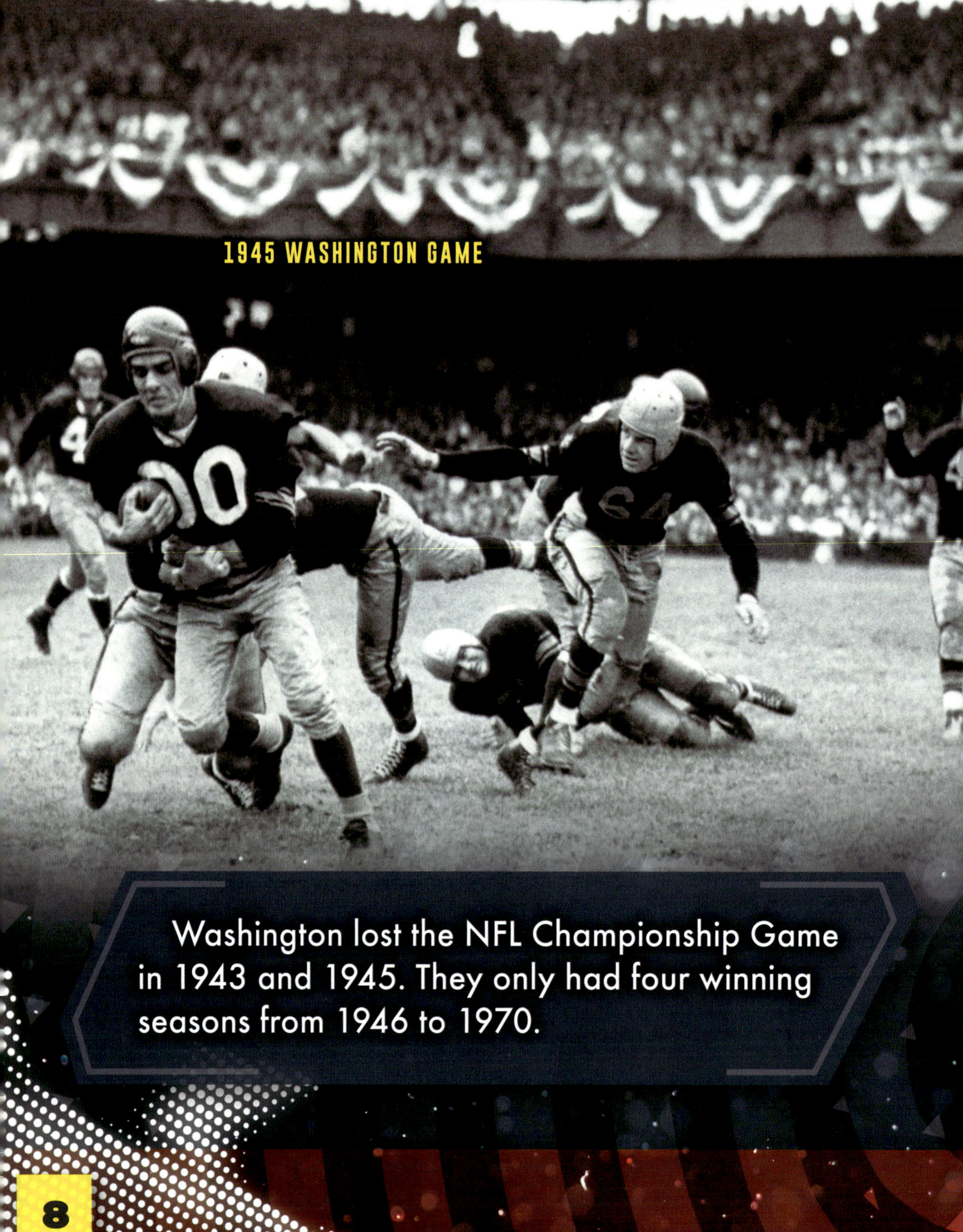

1945 WASHINGTON GAME

Washington lost the NFL Championship Game in 1943 and 1945. They only had four winning seasons from 1946 to 1970.

The team got better in the 1970s. In 1973, the team played in **Super Bowl** 7. But they lost.

SUPER BOWL 7

In 1981, Joe Gibbs became the head coach. He helped the team win its first Super Bowl in 1983.

SUPER BOWL 17

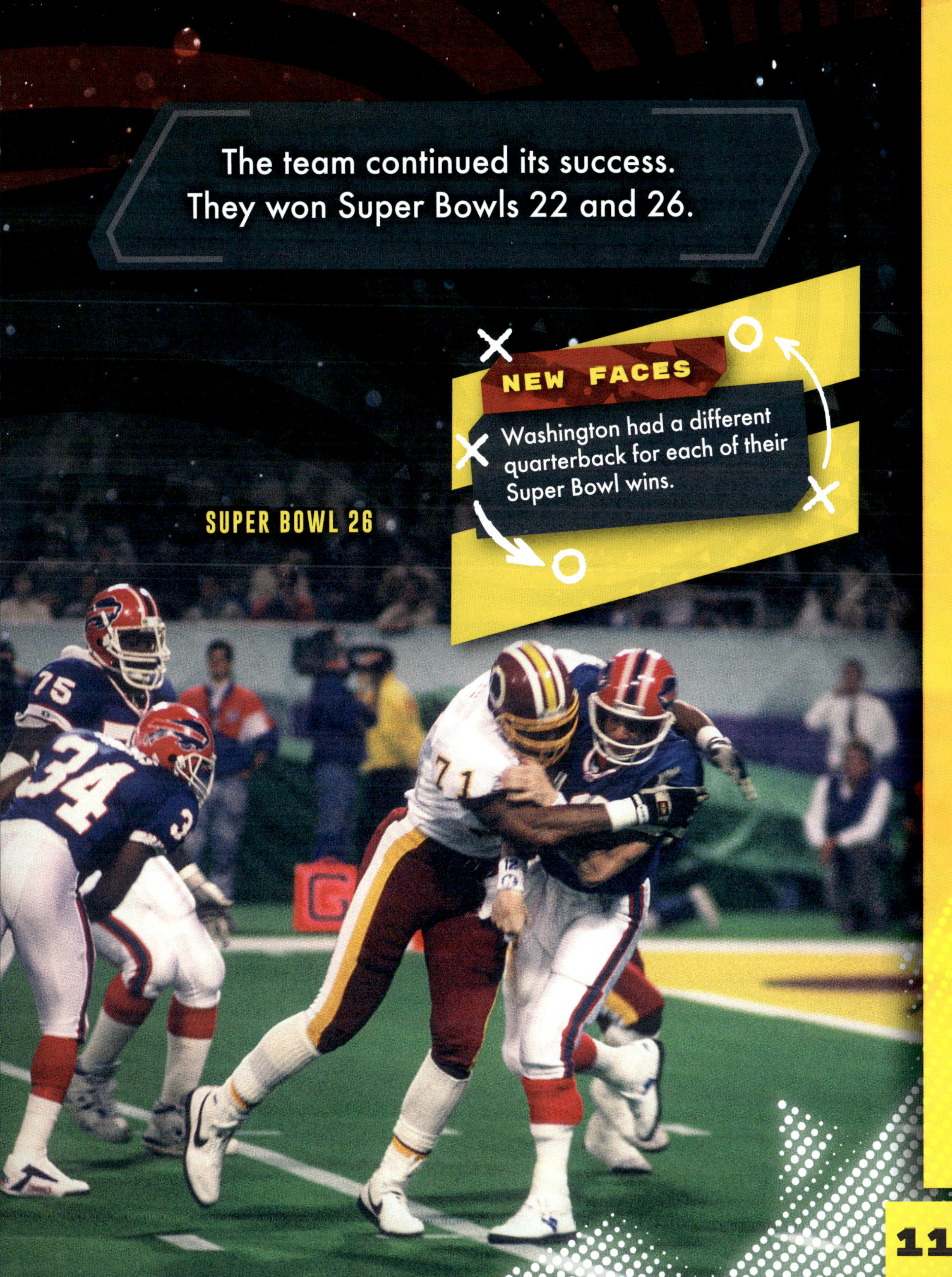

The team continued its success. They won Super Bowls 22 and 26.

## NEW FACES

Washington had a different quarterback for each of their Super Bowl wins.

SUPER BOWL 26

Washington has had many ups and downs since the 1990s. They won their **division** in 2012, 2015, and 2020. But they have not made it far into the **playoffs**.

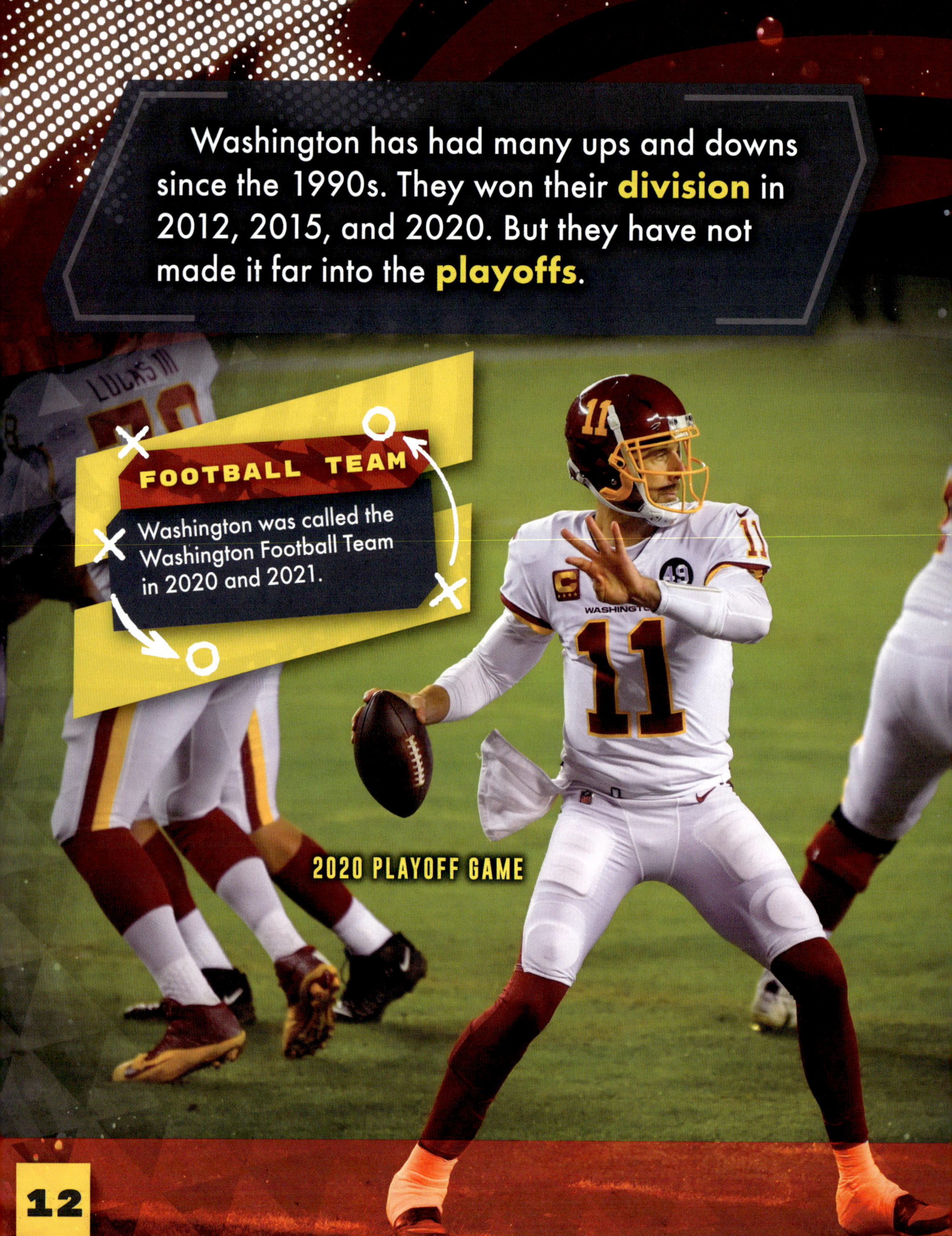

**FOOTBALL TEAM**

Washington was called the Washington Football Team in 2020 and 2021.

2020 PLAYOFF GAME

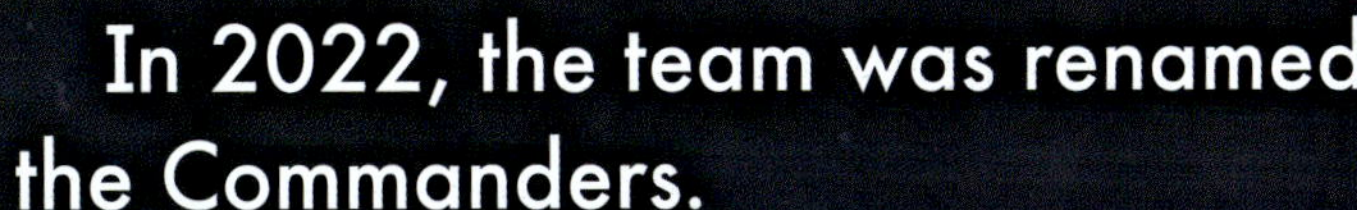
In 2022, the team was renamed the Commanders.

SUPER BOWL
championships
3

# THE COMMANDERS TODAY

COMMANDERS VS. COWBOYS

The Commanders play their home games at FedExField. It is in Landover, Maryland.

The team plays in the NFC East division. The Dallas Cowboys are their biggest **rival**. Another is the New York Giants.

## LOCATION

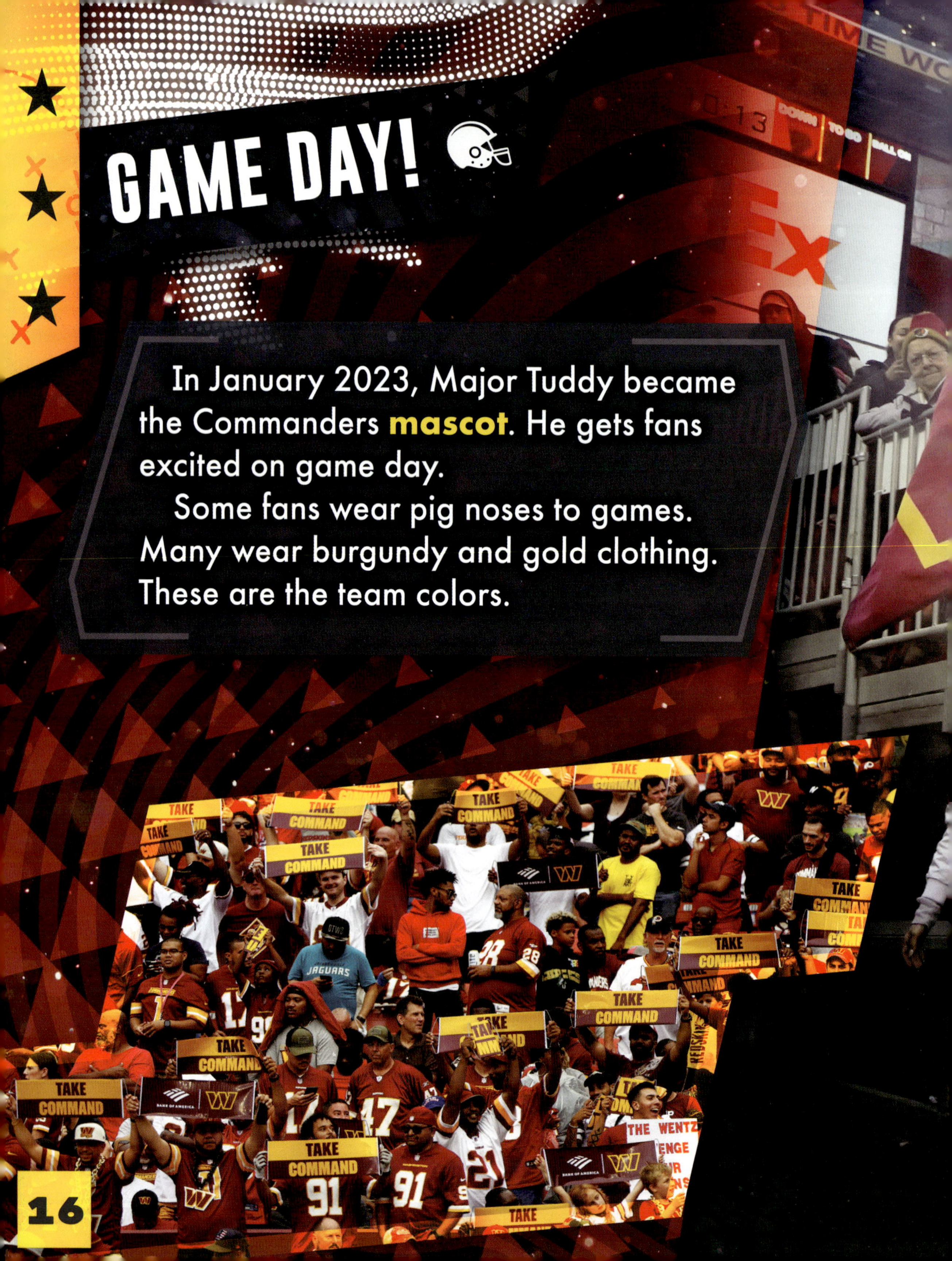

# GAME DAY!

In January 2023, Major Tuddy became the Commanders **mascot**. He gets fans excited on game day.

Some fans wear pig noses to games. Many wear burgundy and gold clothing. These are the team colors.

MAJOR TUDDY

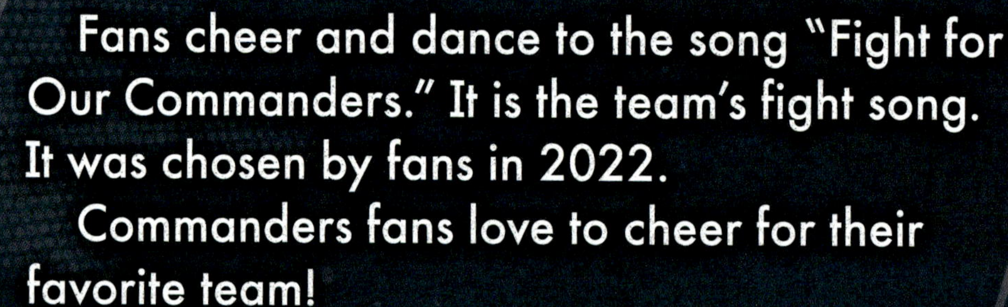

Fans cheer and dance to the song "Fight for Our Commanders." It is the team's fight song. It was chosen by fans in 2022.

Commanders fans love to cheer for their favorite team!

# ★ FAMOUS PLAYERS ★

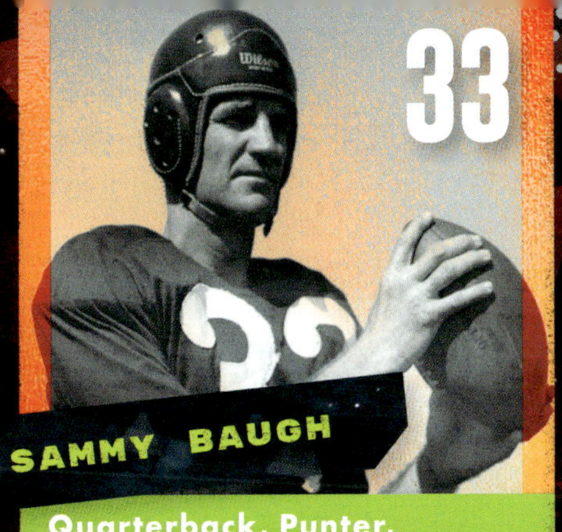


SAMMY BAUGH

Quarterback, Punter, Defensive Back, Running Back

Played 1937–1952

RUSS GRIMM

Guard, Center

Played 1981–1991

SEAN TAYLOR

Defensive Back

Played 2004–2007

ART MONK

Wide Receiver

Played 1980–1993

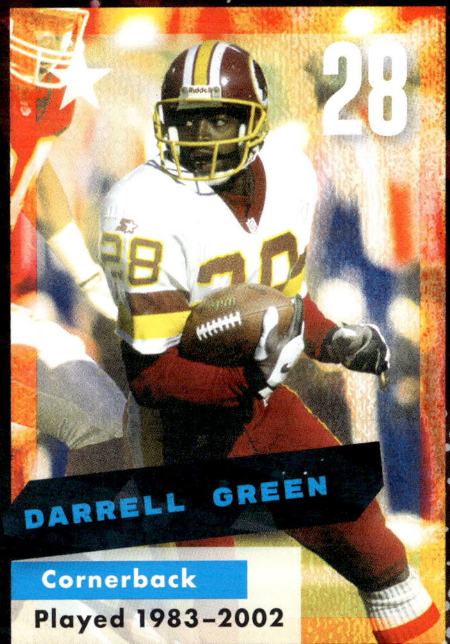


DARRELL GREEN

Cornerback

Played 1983–2002

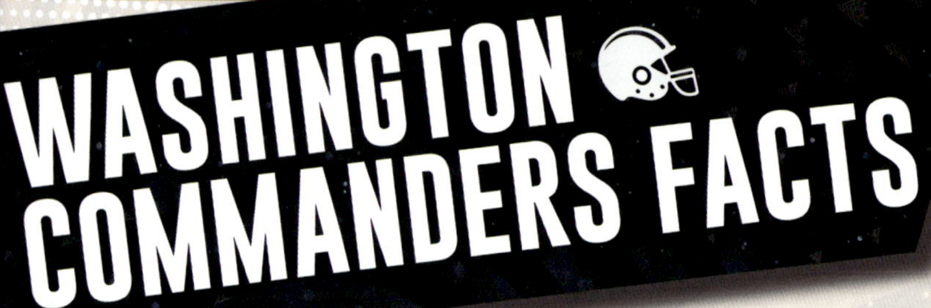

# WASHINGTON COMMANDERS FACTS

LOGO

JOINED THE NFL | 1932

NICKNAME | The Hogs

MASCOT

MAJOR TUDDY

CONFERENCE

National Football Conference (NFC)

COLORS

DIVISION | NFC East

Dallas Cowboys

New York Giants

Philadelphia Eagles

STADIUM

FEDEXFIELD

opened September 14, 1997

holds around 63,000 people

## TIMELINE

**1937**
The team moves to Washington, D.C.

**1983**
Washington wins Super Bowl 17

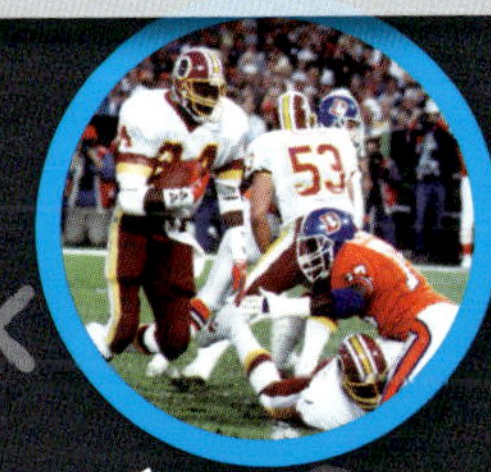

**1988**
Washington wins Super Bowl 22

**1992**
Washington wins Super Bowl 26

**2022**
The team is renamed the Washington Commanders

## ★ RECORDS ★

**All-Time Passing Leader**

Joe Theismann
25,206 yards

**All-Time Rushing Leader**

John Riggins
7,472 yards

**All-Time Receiving Leader**

Art Monk
12,026 yards

**All-Time Scoring Leader**

Mark Moseley
1,206 points

# GLOSSARY

**championship**—a contest to decide the best team or person

**division**—a group of NFL teams from the same area that often play against each other; there are eight divisions in the NFL.

**mascot**—an animal or symbol that represents a sports team

**playoffs**—games played after the regular season is over; playoff games determine which teams play in the championship game.

**quarterback**—a player whose main job is to throw and hand off the ball

**rival**—a long-standing opponent

**Super Bowl**—the annual championship game of the NFL

**touchdown**—a score that occurs when a team crosses into their opponent's end zone with the football; a touchdown is worth six points.

# TO LEARN MORE

## AT THE LIBRARY

Anderson, Josh. *Inside the Washington Commanders.* Minneapolis, Minn.: Lerner Publications, 2024.

Coleman, Ted. *Washington Football Team All-Time Greats.* Mendota Heights, Minn.: Press Box Books, 2022.

Goodman, Michael E. *Washington Commanders.* Mankato, Minn.: Creative Education, 2023.

## ON THE WEB

**FACTSURFER**

Factsurfer.com gives you a safe, fun way to find more information.

1. Go to www.factsurfer.com.
2. Enter "Washington Commanders" into the search box and click 🔍.
3. Select your book cover to see a list of related content.

# INDEX


Boston, Massachusetts, 6
colors, 16, 20
famous players, 19
fans, 16, 18
FedExField, 14, 15, 20
fight song, 18
Gibbs, Joe, 10
Heinicke, Taylor, 4, 5
history, 4, 5, 6, 7, 8, 9, 10, 11, 12, 13, 16, 18
Landover, Maryland, 14, 15
mascot, 16, 17, 20
name, 6, 7, 12, 13
National Football League (NFL), 6, 7, 20
NFC East, 12, 15, 20
NFL championship, 6, 7, 8
playoffs, 12
positions, 5, 11
records, 21
rivals, 15
Super Bowl, 9, 10, 11
timeline, 21
trophy case, 13
Washington, D.C., 6
Washington Commanders facts, 20–21



The images in this book are reproduced through the courtesy of: John Minchillo/ AP Images, cover (hero); Anders Brownworth, cover (stadium); All-Pro Reels/ Wikipedia, pp. 3, 23; Dylan Buell/ Getty, pp. 4-5; Justin Casterline/ Getty, p. 5; ASSOCIATED PRESS/ AP Images, pp. 6, 21 (1937); Bettmann/ Getty, pp. 6-7, 19 (Sammy Baugh); Hall of Fame/ AP Images, pp. 8-9; Focus On Sport/ Getty, pp. 9, 10, 10-11, 21 (1988, Joe Theismann, John Riggins, Art Monk); The Washington Post/ Getty, pp. 12, 21 (2022); Icon Sportswire, p. 14; Ken Howard/ Alamy, p. 15; NFL/ Wikipedia, pp. 15 (Commanders logo), 20 (Commanders logo, Cowboys logo, Giants logo, Eagles logo, NFC logo); Rob Carr/ Getty, p. 16; Jess Rapfogel/ Getty, pp. 16-17; Shaban Athuman/ AP Images, pp. 18-19; Mitchell Layton/ Getty, p. 19 (Art Monk, Sean Taylor); George Gojkovich/ Getty, p. 19 (Russ Grimm); Allen Dean Steele/ Getty, p. 19 (Darrell Green); Aaron M. Sprecher/ AP Images, p. 20 (mascot); Paparacy, p. 20 (stadium); Wally McNamee/ Getty, p. 21 (1983); Diamond Images/ Getty, p. 21 (1992).